I0151464

Moordener Kill

poems by

Paul Genega

Finishing Line Press
Georgetown, Kentucky

Moordener Kill

ACKNOWLEDGMENTS

Grateful acknowledgement to the editors of the following publications where
these poems first appeared, sometimes in earlier forms:

This Broken Shore: Ars Poetica
Descant: Moordener Kill
Evening Street Review: Breakfast with Dorothy and Dick
Free Inquiry: The Day after the Day Lady Di Died
Long Island Quarterly: East End Elegy
Narrative Northeast: In Migration, Dog Aubade
Paterson Literary Review: Memory/Melt/Me, Pearl Become Polly
The Poeming Pigeon: Brown Shirts and Tea
The Stars, edited by Whitney Scott (Dyer, IN, Outrider Press): Stars
Stillwater Review: Conformation
Stone Canoe: Shadow
Tiferet: The Wall

Publisher: Leah Maines
Editor: Christen Kincaid
Cover Art: James Werkowski, *Moordener Kill*
Author Photo: Roy Groething
Cover Design: Elizabeth Maines McCleavy

Printed in the USA on acid-free paper.
Order online: www.finishinglinepress.com
         also available on amazon.com

Author inquiries and mail orders:
Finishing Line Press
P. O. Box 1626
Georgetown, Kentucky 40324
U. S. A.

Table of Contents

Moordener Kill 1

Conformation 3

Brownshirts and Tea 4

Simon of Cyrene 5

The Day After the Day Lady Di Died 6

Pearl Become Polly 8

The Wall 10

East End Elegy 12

In Migration 14

Memory/Melt/Me 15

Breakfast with Dorothy and Dick 16

Dog Aubade 18

Broken Bio 19

Shadow 24

Stars 25

Ars Poetica 26

In the Eye of the Beholder 27

Le Cirque 28

First Kill 30

MOORDENER KILL

moves black in a place which seems sunless
over rock flecked silver white, almost shiny
in the dimness
                over dams of leaf and twig
churn and rush of it dismantling what was
just built

        you can see the creek, one bend
of it at least, from the road which leads
to the ramp which leads to the interstate
which can take you so far west you'll
eventually hit ocean

                        but you can only
see one crook of the creek where you
stand
        like a secret that stays dark
and where it leads
                    eventually you don't
know and don't care
                        content to let it
mumble in the hollow which unlike
the creek is unnamed, unexplored
unloved

except for boys like you were
once, come to linger in the shadows
walking wet stones, laughing, slipping in
spinning
            yarns of graves scooped out
of leaf mold
                  quiet men in white shirts
who dust the world with their trudge
the insatiable hunger of oversalted
childhoods crusted on pink tongues
tales

      to tell and tell and retell until
the telling itself is all you own
the only truth worth telling
the only truth you know—
manifest destiny, memoir, grand guignol

CONFORMATION

for Charles Laughton's Quasimodo
and in memory of my grandparents Ilko and Tessie
who resisted such voices for the sake of their sons

hard chairs bolted to desktops
fixed rows in cold classrooms
the buzz of dying fluorescents

we want the same for our boys
now, nothing modular or mobile
no coddling circles, open skylights

want them to fidget as we did
lust for sun in schoolyards
know how long a minute can

last, boys who will be boys
to carry on as we carried on
as our fathers did, their fathers

sting of wrong answer
slap of disapproval, shame
like wildfire burning its way

from blush to white heat
boys who will brawl into
streets when the bell sounds

sprint to the kingdom of
tilt spin curl lift whirl, there
to crown in our own image

cruel giving way to cool
the next lord of misrule
a new king of fools

BROWN SHIRTS AND TEA:
THE START OF THE PARTY
for Timothy Snyder

Brawled their way into town halls
With the incontrovertible facts
Of their fears, nests of stinging terrors
Sequestered in clenched fists

Cast nets for other in their midst
Color wrong other, language wrong
Other, wrong prayers—poxes
Curdling dreams of pure power

Freed from inconveniences
Like history or heart, thus
To write with unchecked might
An epic revision of the land

There then, the darkness was loosed
Here now, its reknotting noose

SIMON OF CYRENE

He's the biblical prophet of New Criticism no history
no bio no record how or why he trekked from
North Africa to. Jerusalem he's just there
plucked from anonymity by a party of centurions
and handed the heavy cross to bear chosen
some say for the warm wet of his eyes trembling
bit lip while others less romantic view the man
like me alone in a strange city blinded by
noon sun desert dry mouth worrying remnants
of a prayer his entry into history less empathy
than irony the last literary skill that we learn

though learned it was well-learned by a group
of ancient Gnostics who believed (divine flesh
being illusory) it was Simon not Jesus
affixed to that cross switched at the crunch
when bile and blood and a body to abandon
mattered more than props the passion
in essence another tabloid case of identity
mistaken a twisted Hitchcock plot proof if
proof was needed the death penalty should die

that mystic take however a decidedly unpopular
position most seeing the Cyrenean as the ideal
Everyman a supporting role at best played
on stage by Robeson in film by Poitier
as if only a Black man could presto
save the Deus salvage the salvation
come through in a pinch as if all the heavy
lifting rendered this land our land holy
as if justice and truth were the MacGuffin

THE DAY AFTER THE DAY LADY DI DIED

I wish I could say I was seated at my desk
behind a stack of papers so preternaturally smart
my red pen hadn't moved
                              or was lost in a poem
by Kenneth Patchen, May Swenson or Sarton
some other voice or vision I feared the canon
might soon lose
                      but it was a hot September 1st
fall semester just begun, and having given myself
the gift of skipping the first meeting of the General
Education Oversight Committee
                                      I was almost
out the door, mere minutes left to office hours
straight up rye Manhattan buzzing my dry tongue
when she walked in
                          a face without a name
recalled vaguely from last spring, and though
tempted to report I'd just received an urgent message
from the provost
                      or more urgently, she who purveys
our parking decals, there was something in her *hey*
part North Ward part Bacall, in the raggedy red
of her eyes, which
                          made me stop, pull up a chair and
ask almost in church whisper what was on her mind
to which, hard sighing, she replied in a rush of sodden
vowels was the death
                          the day before of Lady Di
in Paris in a race with those Furies of glitz, the paparazzi
prompting her to wonder through a sleepless night
of sobs what symbol

portent, semaphore or sign
could be found in that crash, what secrets we might glean
from a limo's twisted steel, what it all meant—in other words
assurance the happily
ever afters she'd been raised on
were still real, that was what she'd come for, what her
soft raw eyes implored as I scratched chin, cracked
knuckles, waited
until my words wrung of old tears
rang true to explain that as I saw it sometimes… maybe
probably… perhaps… it was good to take one's foot
off the accelerator.

PEARL BECOME POLLY

In the thinnest years of the Depression
Pearl sent a postcard from the Catskills
to my grandmother—*Come quick, Rose*
she wrote in spindly blue script
There is plenty plenty food here

Rose, Pearl and a steerage hold of
cousins had fled the flocked parchment
that was Europe on the cusp of WWI
sloshed across with *Norddeutscher*
from Bremen, landed in Ludlow Street

tenements and survived—married worked
skimped bore, retiring at last in widow black
swimsuits in the land of palmetto palms
and limes, where Pearl, reborn as Polly
still simmering soup left on mama's stove

organized excursions to allyoucaneat
earlybirdspecialseniorcitizendiscount
cafeterias dressed in polyester best
red lipstick daubed on left front tooth
piling trays high with all that history

and circumstance had deprived
choppedliverbeetsaladdillcucumber
ricepilafhushpuppiesbutterbeanschicken
kievtetrazinniapplepiepumpkinpie
lemonmeringuemince and one fateful

July night a sliver of pecan à la mode
that sliver alas proving fatal, catching
in throat, clinging, a lifetime
of want and fear of want rising
behind the clipped hibiscus rising

the need for more—moremoremore
and more—Aunt Pearl become Polly
strangled by her hunger, an emptiness
so deep so insistent so insatiable so sad
she could have been America itself

THE WALL

There's the remnant of a wall in the woods
I like to walk when the curtain of sleep rises early

Stones long ago toppled from places they fit tightly
Lay scattered in dimness daubed with lichen and moss

Some lean over like inebriated choristers
Others lay flat on their worm-riddled backs
Gazing up at the unblinking moon

There's no hint of what was walled in or walled out

No scar patch of pasture where vine and nettle thrive
No telling shards of cow horn or sheep jaw

The wall stands roughly three feet high
Though its height seems less important
Than the breadth of its arc

Glacial rubble stretching out on umber
Silvered at sunrise by spider web and dew

The land looks all of a piece at the moment
But once, this wall insists, it was parceled
And divided, strictly cordoned by purpose and deed

On one side was something called mine
On the other yours or everyone's or no one's

Hills prairies meadows ravines
Whitewater surging freely to the sea

There and then and here and now

Before there was a then and now
Before the gods bed down in leaf mold
Before the wall builders set sail

EAST END ELEGY
for A.K.

the pink of our teens
had long ago popped

consuming passions
burnt down to nostalgia

era of firsts behind us
marriages, jobs, failures

we fit at last the raggedy
costume called self

*

in a dimming afternoon
summerscape we trudged

the lip of a sand bluff
pausing to gaze out

on Cedar Point, Maidstone,
Gardiners Bay, Shelter Island

in the amethyst distance
Orient, disease-frizzed Plum

*

lee path choked with grape vine
bittersweet, pitch pine, rose

windward, sheer drop
to a shell encrusted beach

blackbacks, scoters, plovers
ancient skiff with rusted oarlocks

splintered starboard gunwale
fisherwind rising for to ferry us away

*

all this long ago, before
the potato fields were blighted

before the hypno-rich arrived
to claim the sea as their mirror

but I see us again there
and then, see how young

we were without knowing it
how happy, without a clue

*

how beautiful that day
that shimmering stretch

of sea sand, perched high
on the shifting lip of it

the silence sweet and salty
with all the time in the world

to say what needed to be said
all the time that never was

IN MIGRATION

Inside mud skin
heavy winter

run-off quickens
the creek into

small walls
of froth

wet-footed
forest offering up

skunk cabbage
anemones

the seductive
blush of vines

A phoebe calls
from budding

alder where
one year ago

today stretched
over the sibilance

I held a wake
on the water

and let fly
my sister's ashes

MEMORY / MELT / ME

Grandmother took me from
The stubbly yawn of the suburbs

To Manhattan. We climbed rocks
In Central Park, caught a movie

At the Roxy, ate chop suey.
By the time I turned around

That black and white city
Had vanished, just like her.

Today a mid-March blizzard
Buries each and all, the living

And the gone. I can hear her
Now declaiming how *raptorous*

This snow—flakes after erasure
Currier & Ives. But even come

Late Easter mounds of gray will
Still flank the Walmart parking lot.

   The past falls from the place
   Where time has flown—

   A slow drip on slick asphalt
   A flurry of white lies.

BREAKFAST WITH DOROTHY AND DICK

Dorothy Kilgallen and husband Richard
Kollman's morning radio show, broadcast
on WOR-AM, New York, 1945-1963

Long ago in seersucker pajamas
In a small suburban cape, I soaked in
Your every word—learned, even more critical
Than meaning, the way each word should be said
Which syllables received heavy breath, broad
Vowels, the meaningful emphasis or pause.
You were the ultimate Manhattan sophisticates
Dishing out reviews, nightclub news, gossip
Last night's Broadway opening featuring
Folks every bit as *au courant* as you
Pulling up to the Booth in shiny Checker cabs
Only rendered shinier and more precious
If it rained. I sat with bated breath as if
I were a backer as *The Telegraph* or *Times*
Opined thumbs up
                    or down. O Dorothy O Dick
In your smart black dresses and three piece suits
Ensconced in your neo-Georgian brownstone
Served coddled eggs and buttered toast
By your genial butler Julius, you made me believe
Couples started each morning with *Hello darling*
Hello sweetie. Made me believe in a city that
Wore a necklace nightly of tourmaline and pearl
An America with one extended pinky
Cole Porter tunes tinkling in the background
Something rose-colored fizzy in a flute
An America of Americans who parlezed French
Smoked cigarettes from meerschaum holders
Tossed silver fox stoles over the right shoulder
An America of the best and brightest smiles
That met beneath the Biltmore's gleaming clock
The flesh of a dream that did not include boys

Who shopped the husky racks at Ohrbach's
Didn't know a sarabande from a samba
Had never kvelled over sweetbreads or snails
The movers and shakers of a set so posh and
Precious I would someday come to realize
They were just too fucking chichi to be me.

DOG AUBADE

The doe scissors
away from us

you, as always
a yard or two ahead

free of the lead
gay tail waving

Not so shy
these deer fly

orbiting our heads
like hungry halos

I swat
You sprint

At the far end
of the field

fawns slip
through silver birch

The sun rises
A welt rises

Crushed flies
stud my matted hair

BROKEN BIO

Like a slow drip IV, so much of me seems to come from him—scowl, sneer, frown, pout, glower, grimace... short fused rage...

Also, sense of self in the enormous, love of language, faith in facts...

Khrushchev, whom he resembled, made him smile.

Hitchcock, whom he resembled even more, grandmother called "boyfriend" when his moon-belly profile eclipsed the tv screen, the kind of offhand comment dissidents let slip in totalitarian regimes, flagrant but unassailable, too slyly polite for plodding literalists.

Meet the Press was his sole religion Sunday mornings though he was dressed in his best, pipe tight in clenched teeth, long before the sun rose.

Once, I was told, and told and told so often I sometimes remember being there, my parents were late for noon dinner.

Five minutes late... ten minutes... fifteen... full half hour... at which point he rose from his chair, smashed every plate on the table.

Breakage, fracture, splinter, dislocation... these are the things he was made of.

The youngest of eight his widowed mother brought to America in that great wash of immigration before the First World War.

When he was fifteen he fell and broke both arms.

Unable to work or care for himself, he was shunted for months from one married sibling to the next.

Every brother and sister and their spouses groused loudly.

Complained they didn't have enough for themselves and their kids.

Said they were too tired to take on more.

Begrudged him every crumb.

Neither bones nor bonds ever healed completely.

But he was the only one of that generation in the family to finish high school.

Then opened and closed and opened and closed and opened and closed businesses in every borough of New York.

Made the family move whenever he changed business.

Had to walk home for lunch.

Refused to eat leftovers, even in the tightest years of the Depression.

And more often than not, whenever he switched businesses, he changed his surname as well.

Breakage, fracture, splinter, dislocation… these are the traits passed from him to mother to me.

After fifty years of terror, my grandmother finally filed for divorce, swallowing a vial of white and purple pills.

She is buried beside my aunt on a wind worn knoll in Oklahoma.

He is interred somewhere in south Florida.

I've often wondered if there is a cross on his stone, what name has been chiseled.

If I had my way, it would read

William _____
Everyone Was Scared of Him

Especially his daughters, who felt his hand if they bawled.

Although always flush with cash, he wouldn't lend my father a dime to start a camera shop (where one opened and flourished) or an ice cream stand (where one sprang up and still thrives) yet would show up at our doorstep with chops so thick they could be roasts, or take us out for a dinner costing more than my father brought home in a week.

The grand gesture, big show.

He was very Slavic that way.

Once, when I was little, I got a doctor kit for Christmas, waddled up to him, and rammed the thermometer up his rear.

He jumped.

Yawped.

Smiled like Nikita.

But I did not feel his hand.

Then later—after I'd grown darker, more miserably alone—he would take me every summer for a day of fishing on Great South Bay.

Up before dawn, admonished to be ready, how he wouldn't wait if I wasn't.

A silent drive in the dark.

The lapping black as we waited to board the boat—

where all glorious day long I was allowed anything I wanted… grape soda and cheese doodles for breakfast… ice cream and Cracker Jacks for lunch.

There was always a pool for the biggest fish caught and the mate would ask if I was to be included.

"The boy's in," he would say, skinning a fat wad of bills.

He never made me feel like a mincing sissy kid.

Not ever.

"The boy's in," he would say, taking a nip from his hip flask.

He was as good at catching fish as he was at making money.

Sometimes he hauled home so many he couldn't give them all away, even after cleaning—slicing off the heads, scooping out the viscera, tossing the guts onto a backyard patch of vegetables.

The neighborhood cats all adored him.

The day he died my mother and father were flying down to Florida to visit for the first time in years.

The neighbors reported that an ambulance that morning had been called by the woman he was living with—a woman my parents never met but who sent flowers to the funeral From a Friend.

By then I was working for Billboard in Manhattan, learning how downright idiotic capitalism really was.

When my mother called to tell what had happened, I gave myself the day off.

All I could think was the black lap of waves.

The way he'd say, "the boy's in."

My mouth so slick with salt and sugar it went numb.

I spent the afternoon alone wandering through drizzle, trawling for men near the Central Park lake.

Something in my blood so cavernously, ravenously hungry that it stang.

The day stretched out...

Mist darkened into rage...

But I kept on... kept on moving.

I wanted to find love.

Wanted to put him in his place.

SHADOW

On a brilliant
April morning

when I look down
at the shadow

I am walking
on a coltsfoot

lined brick path
it surprises

me to see my
grandfather's skull

Munch's silent scream
his largely deaf

florets of ears
where I should be

STARS

The famous writer referenced the Ronettes
in his work so after the reading I stood
on line to tell him that Ronnie Spector
years ago had been a neighbor on West End
& how one wet Thanksgiving eve heading
off to watch the big balloons get blown up
for the parade she'd knocked on the door
coyly smiling, asked to score a cup
of Stoly, then recumbent on the couch
held forth nearly until dawn—a star
in a blue silk slit skirt, humming with
the Beatles, headlining for the Stones.

It was a favorite story, one I was eager
to retell, when halfway into *Spec*-tor
I watched famous writer's baby blues
glaze to bacon grease, balloon over his head
wondering if I'd make him late for moonrise
or whatever celestial event had been arranged
& it was then that I knew what I always
should have known, some memories, like most
dreams, are better kept than told, fade as fast
as gemstones plucked from the sea's song—
like *the night we met...* like *walking in
the rain...* like this *whoa-oh-oh-oh* poem.

ARS POETICA

Arrangement in Black and Gold
Comte Robert de Montesquiou-Fezensac, 1891-92,
James McNeill Whistler, The Frick Collection, New York

Wearing the night
He steps out of it

Right foot forward
Elegant and arched

Face sculpted
By fragile hauteur

Mask he can slip
On, fall into, bear

Scarred hands, their
Insolent geography

Secreted away in
White sateen sheen

One holds his *badine*
The other a chinchilla

Skin of yet another
Weary evening out

Pose, performance
Gesture, implication

Actor in and of a set
Laced with violets

And pralines he is
Carapace encrusted with

The jewels of Ali Baba
Lord of prepositions

The thing… the thing
Itself, himself, a poem

IN THE EYE OF THE BEHOLDER
Marsden Hartley's Maine
Met Breuer, New York, June, 2017

a mess a mess
the navy clad
critic mumbles
pointing to a jumble
of lumber on a creek

    and this one
    well he sniffs
    the hunky
    hirsute Quebecois
    simply not his taste

        ditto with
        tiered steeple
        rope duck shell
        tinker mackerel
        lighthouse whipped by waves

    then freeze framed
    at the exit
    by flat top Mount
    Katahdin fraught
    with white in a storm

at last he cries
thin lips blooming
a painting
worth the bother of
eavesdroppers and crowds

        the perfect
        peony
        caught in oil
        icy cultivar
        Duchesse de Nemours

LE CIRQUE

Georges Seurat, 1890-91, Musée D'Orsay, Paris

wednesday   evening   at Cirque Fernando   the dark
ringmaster   sleek as an eel   in his tux   exhorts
the Mazepa rider   to rise   she lifts   on left leg

without   saddle   or reins   arms   arcing
as   the somersaulting   acrobat   arcs   white
steed's slender   neck   the wide curve   of the ring

sparse   crowd   rigidly   cordoned   by class
and by   caste :   compère   wannabes   in cutaways
have   their own   section   proper   families

sporting   bowlers   and bonnets   comprise   a
larger   middle   tier   and above them   at the top
in an emptier   airier   realm   two men   ignore

the hubbub   below   engaged   in a tense   bland
conversation   they   could be   Groucho and Chico
Estrogen   and Vladimir   Leopold and   Loeb

any unfinished dialectic :   the crux   of their dispute
is   the future   the new century   fast approaching
about which   they   know   as little   as   the

whitefaced   clown   greased   and agape   red
cap   and   fringed   shirt   flowing   knows much :
midnight   trains   grinding   their teeth   across

black   steppes   steeped   in cold   the brute
brute   march   of boots   landscape   of shudders
slaughterhouse   of isms   still   life   of   ash :

this is what   Medrano   sees   in the center   of the
circus   at the corner   of Martyrs   and Rochechanut
the vision   his laugh   paints   on a plank   of bad

air   on which   he must   insist   though   it's
not   what   Seurat   wants   from   this   raucous
evening   out   this   tumbling   and   trembling

this   opus   left   undone :   passionate   divisionism
chromoluminarism   art   rendered   scientific
objectivized   precise :   like history   says   the clown

like famine   says   the clown   why   we   cry

FIRST KILL

Rocks and heavy clay. Not good for much they say but some
raggedy-ass vegetables. Truth is, I've never starved—
snow peas carrots cabbage squash, plus the pigs and chickens.
Lean years, yes—floods, drought. And once a rain-haired twister
rage chasing its tail, pulling up roots like a mad god. But mostly

it's been this—meadow spikes after a spring shower
opening in copper scarlet teal—drifts of fresh green on a rise—
the crook of a kill dreaming through black willow, so clear
and cool at sunrise a man can stand himself again. I've pulled

myself from that white-throated gurgle more times
than I remember after a hard drunk. And drunk I have been
plenty—slumped over the table talking with the demons
taking shots and talking, talking shots and taking, until
I finally outdrink them, till they finally pass out. I've known

those two so long it amazes I can't name them.
Truth is, I cannot. Only know the day I was told to get going
when I packed my things and got, they were right behind me
snarling and sneering down the snaking road. They're

the bad dogs of the air during the day, invisible
as wind over packed ground, but I can tell their doing—
placing hammer on top finger, burning up the sausages
switching lefts with rights. Nights they take shape clearly
not visible like spoons—they fill dark spaces darkly—

but present as last spring, talking talking talking
how I put in seeds too shallow too early too late
how I will starve should starve must starve, is my fate—
talking talking their quiet grammatical hate. Sometimes

I watch sky boil into night, look out on the garden
the stand of pine I put down as saplings, and I whisper
to my good hound, yes, you're right, in the main
we did all right. Then I hear a crow cry, watch
a feisty little sparrow beleaguer the fiend from its nest

and I wish I was more like that. Am not. And cannot be.
Still, if Jesus, as they say found himself lost forty long days
in the desert with the devil I can nearly match him
day for year, wasteland tract for fertile field. His

choked with dust, sing the visions and strictures
only sun-stabbed barrens spawn. But mine—
attention mine—lit with jealousy and promise are
lapped by the babble of Eden's feeding streams. And
mine, God damn it—see the gauzing—mine are green.

Paul Genega is the author of six full-length collections of poetry and five chapbooks. His latest, *Sculling on the Lethe,* was published by Salmon Poetry, Ireland, in 2018 and was a Finalist for the Eugene Paul Nassar Poetry Prize. Over a forty year career, his work has appeared in a wide range of journals and magazines including *Poetry, North American Review, Kansas Quarterly, Epoch* and *Narrative Northeast* and in anthologies such as *Like Light* (Bright Hill Press) and *Dogs Singing: A Tribute Anthology* (Salmon). His work has received such honors as the Lucille Medwick Award (*New York Quarterly*), The Discovery Award (*The Nation*), Charles Angoff Award (*The Literary Review*), the Allen Ginsberg Award (Honorable Mention, *Paterson Literary Review*) and an individual fellowship from the National Endowment for the Arts. His poetry is also featured in the multi-media theater piece *Paging Doctor Faustus*, which was presented in a workshop production at FiveMyles Gallery, Brooklyn, in April, 2019, and in the play *Ophelia Comes to Brooklyn* by Katja Dryer, which premiered in Brussels, spring 2018. *Perhaps*, a collaborative portfolio of poems with original etchings by Boston artist Aaron Fink, is in the permanent collections of the National Gallery, the Harvard Museums, and the Block Museum at Northwestern, among others. Genega taught for many years at Bloomfield College, New Jersey—one of the most diverse private colleges in the Northeast—where he founded the creative writing program and served as both Chair of Humanities and Chair of Faculty. His legacy continues at Bloomfield through the Genega Endowed Scholarships in Creative Writing. He lives on the edge of the mighty Hudson in Stuyvesant, New York with his husband Jim and their Welsh Springer Spaniel Chance.

www.ingramcontent.com/pod-product-compliance
Lightning Source LLC
LaVergne TN
LVHW051612080426
835510LV00020B/3254